The Conflict Resolution Library™

Dealing with Insults
Qué hacer con los insultos

Marianne Johnston

Traducción al español:
Mauricio Velázquez de León

PowerKiDS press & Editorial Buenas Letras™
New York

Published in 2008 by The Rosen Publishing Group, Inc.
29 East 21st Street, New York, NY 10010

First Bilingual Edition

Book Design: Lissette González

Photo Credits: Cover photo © Carri Keill/iStockphoto; p. 15 by Maria Moreno; all other photos by Thomas Mangieri.

Cataloging Data

Johnston, Marianne.
   Marianne Johnston / Dealing with insults; traducción al español: Mauricio Velázquez
   de León.
   p. cm. – (Conflict Resolution Library/Biblioteca solución de conflictos)
Includes index.
   ISBN-13: 978-1-4042-7661-1 (library binding)
   ISBN-10: 1-4042-7661-0 (library binding)
1. Verbal self-defense–Juvenile literature. 2. Invective–Juvenile literature. [1. Verbal self-defense. 2. Invective. 3. Spanish language materials.] I. Title. II. Series.

Manufactured in the United States of America

Contents

Contenido

Insults are words used to hurt other people. People who insult others usually don't feel good about themselves. They may be angry, or they may not know how to talk about their feelings in a helpful way.

Los insultos son palabras que se usan para herir a las personas. Generalmente, quienes insultan a otras personas no se sienten muy bien consigo mismos. Quizás están enojados con los demás, o no saben cómo hablar de sus emociones.

5

Maybe when your brother turned off the TV while you were watching it you called him a jerk. That is an insult, and insults hurt other people. Insults don't tell the person what you really mean. All they do is hurt people's feelings.

Estás viendo televisión y tu hermano la apaga. Entonces le dices que es un idiota. Eso es un insulto, y los insultos hieren a los demás. Los insultos no le dicen a la otra persona lo que le quieres decir. Lo único que hacen es herir sus sentimientos.

When someone insults you, your first thought may be to insult him or her right back. Don't do it. Think about why the person is insulting you. Is he angry with you, or is he just being mean?

Cuando alguien te insulta, quizás lo primero que piensas es en insultarlo tú también. No lo hagas. Piensa por qué te está insultando. ¿Está enojado o sólo se está haciendo el malvado?

People who insult others don't feel good about themselves. They have low **self-esteem**. A good way to deal with insults is to build up your own self-esteem. If you believe in yourself, insults from other people don't hurt so much.

Las personas que insultan a otras no se sienten muy bien consigo mismas. Tienen baja **autoestima**. Una buena forma de lidiar con los insultos es desarrollar tu autoestima. Si crees en ti mismo, los insultos de otras personas no te lastimarán tanto.

If you have a brother or sister, you may spend a lot of time together. You may start to **annoy** each other. Instead of insulting each other, spend some time away from each other. When you've both calmed down, you can talk and work the problem out.

Si tienes un hermano o hermana, es probable que pasen mucho tiempo juntos. Después de un rato quizás comienzan a **fastidiarse**. En lugar de insultarse, sepárense un rato. Cuando se hayan calmado, podrán hablar del problema.

13

Luz asked her sister, Ana, a question Ana couldn't answer. Luz became angry and called Ana "stupid." This hurt Ana's feelings. Later that day, Luz **apologized** to Ana. Ana accepted her apology, and the insult was forgiven.

Luz le hizo una pregunta a su hermana Ana que no pudo responder. Luz se enojó y le dijo que era una tonta. Esto hirió los sentimientos de Ana. Más tarde, Luz se **disculpó** con su hermana. Ana aceptó la disculpa y el insulto quedó olvidado.

When strangers or **bullies** insult you, they want you to insult them back. The best way to deal with bullies is to ignore them. They will realize that you are not going to give them what they want, and they will leave you alone.

Cuando un extraño o un **bravucón** te insultan, lo que quieren es que les devuelvas el insulto. La mejor manera de tratar a un bravucón es ignorándolo. Así se dará cuenta de que no le darás lo que quiere, y te dejará en paz.

Insults are hardest to deal with when they come from friends. If a friend insults you often, think about what kind of friend you have. Good friends don't make a habit of insulting each other.

Es más difícil manejar los insultos cuando vienen de nuestros amigos. Si un amigo te insulta con frecuencia, piensa qué clase de amigo tienes. Los buenos amigos no hacen un hábito de insultarse.

Alicia and Vicky had an argument about sharing Alicia's bike. Vicky called Alicia selfish. Alicia called Vicky a spoiled brat. Vicky got angry. The next day, the girls talked without insulting each other. They both said they were sorry.

Alicia y Vicky tuvieron una discusión acerca de la bicicleta de Alicia. Vicky le dijo a Alicia que era una egoísta. Alicia le dijo a Vicky que era una consentida. Vicky se enojó. Al día siguiente, hablaron sin insultarse. Ambas dijeron que lo sentían mucho.

Do you know the saying, "Sticks and stones can break my bones, but names can never hurt me"? Words hurt you only if you let them. The person who really has a problem is the one who insults others, not the person who is insulted.

¿Conoces el refrán que dice "A palabras necias oídos sordos"? Las palabras sólo pueden herirte si tú lo permites. La persona que realmente tiene un problema es la que insulta, no la persona que es insultada.

Glossary

annoy (a-NOY) To disturb or bother a person.

apologize (a-POL-o-jize) To say, "I'm sorry."

bullies (BUL-lee) People who make other people feel bad on purpose.

self-esteem (SELF-es-TEEM) What you think about yourself.

Glosario

autoestima (la) Lo que piensas de ti mismo.

bravucón (-a) Persona que hace sentirse mal a otros a propósito.

disculparse Decir "Lo siento" o "Perdóname".

fastidiar Cuando molestamos a otra persona.

Index

Índice